Farm Machines At Work

Milking Machines

By Hal Rogers

The Child's World.

Published by The Child's World®, Inc.

Design and Production:
The Creative Spark, San Juan Capistrano, CA

Photos: © 1999 David M. Budd Photography

Library of Congress Cataloging-in-Publication Data

Rogers, Hal, 1966-
        Milking machines / by Hal Rogers.
            p. cm.
        Summary: Describes the machines that are used to milk cows and goats on modern farms.
        ISBN 1-56766-753-8 (lib. bdg. : alk. paper)
        1. Milking machines—Juvenile literature. [1. Milking machines. 2. Agricultural machinery.]
    I. Title.

SF247 .R64 2000
637'.124'0284--dc21
                                                                                        99-089470

Contents

On the Job   **4**

Come Inside!   **20**

Up Close   **22**

Glossary   **24**

On the Job

On the job, **dairy** farmers use milking machines to milk cows. These machines look like the one in the top photo. Before there were milking machines, farmers milked cows by hand. The little boy in the bottom photo is learning how to milk a cow at a state fair.

4

This **milking parlor** is inside a big barn. The cows wait outside until it is their turn to be milked.

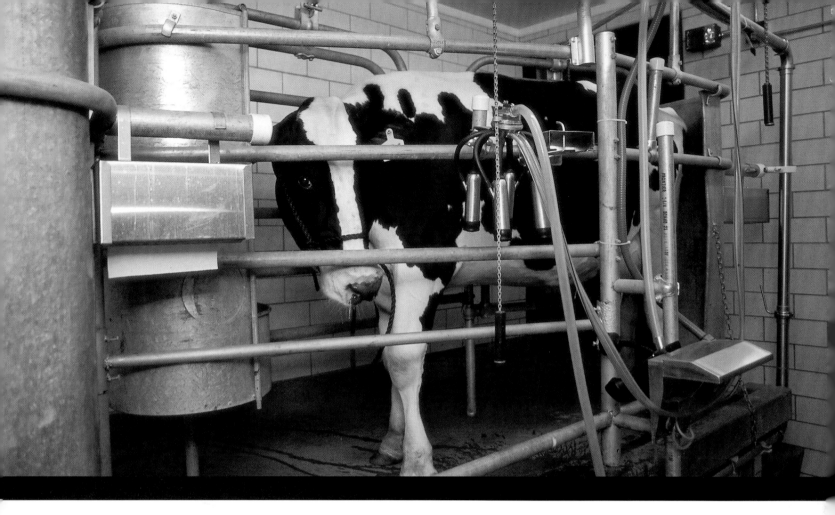

The farmer brings each cow into a **stall.**

The stall helps keep the cow from moving

too much. Here comes the cow!

The milk is inside the cow's **udder.** The milk comes out of the **teats.** The farmer cleans the teats with **iodine.** This helps keep the milk clean. Next, the farmer attaches **teat cups** to the teats.

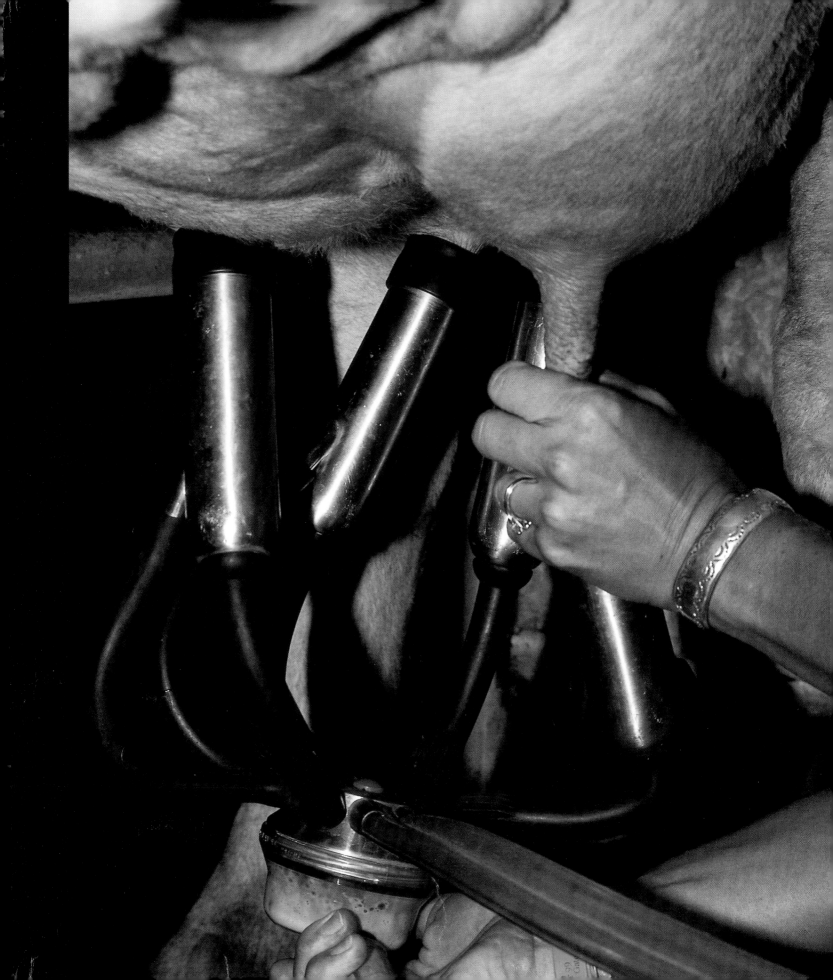

This milking parlor has many **hoses** and

pipes. Milk flows through the teat cups

and into a hose. Then it travels through

a pipe and into big **tanks.**

Milk can only stay in the tanks for a short time. Otherwise, it spoils. The farmer sells the milk to a company where it will be **pasteurized.**

Soon the cow's udder is empty. The farmer walks her out of the milking parlor.

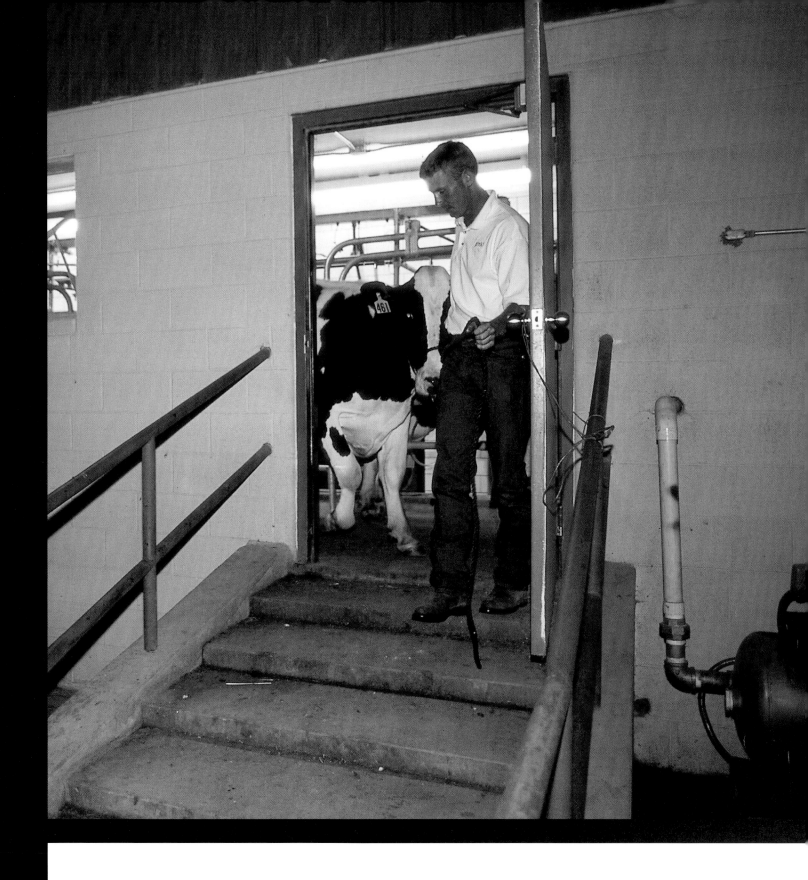

Now it is time to clean up! The farmer
keeps the milking machine and the
parlor clean.

It looks like someone spilled some milk!

The farmer's cat helps clean up, too.

Farmers can also use milking machines with other animals. Goats' milk is used to make cheese.

Come Inside!

Come inside the milking parlor! Do you want to help the farmer?

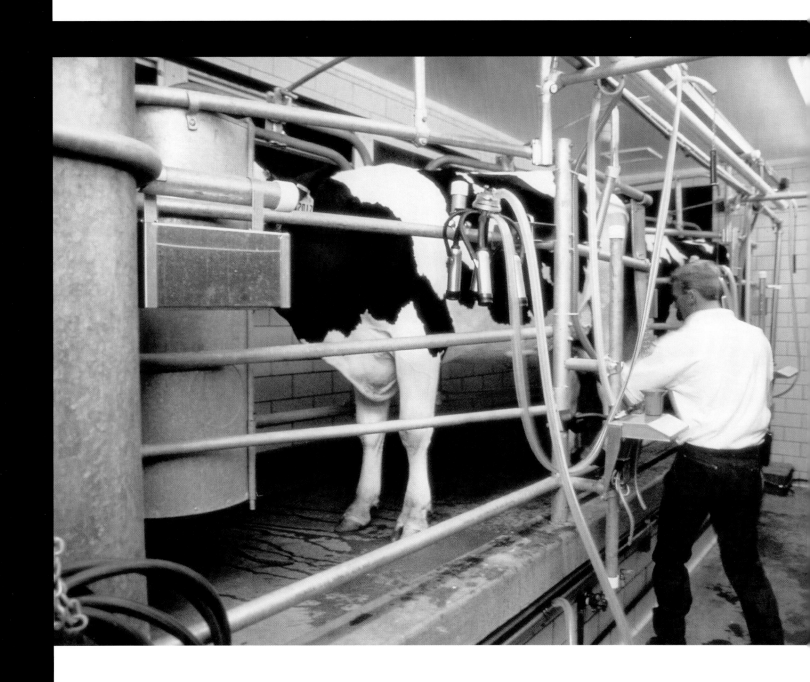

Up Close

1. The udder

2. The teat cups

3. The hoses

4. The tanks

5. The pipes

6. The stall

Glossary

dairy (DARE-ee)
A dairy is a farm where animals are raised to produce milk. Cows' milk comes from a dairy farm.

hoses (HOH-zez)
Hoses are long tubes that can move something wet. A milking machine has many hoses.

iodine (EYE-eh-dyne)
Iodine is a brownish-red liquid that kills germs. Dairy farmers clean their cows' teats with iodine.

milking parlor (MILK-ing PAR-lor)
A milking parlor is a big room where a farmer milks cows. Milking parlors are often inside barns.

pasteurized (PAS-che-ryzd)
If milk is pasteurized, it is heated. Heat kills germs that may be in milk.

pipes (PYPZ)
Pipes are tubes that liquids flow through. A milking machine has many pipes.

stall (STAWL)
A stall is a small place for an animal inside a barn. Cows are put in stalls while they are being milked to keep them from moving too much.

tanks (TANGKS)
Tanks are large containers for liquids. At a dairy farm, milk is stored in tanks.

teat cups (TEET KUPS)
Teat cups are part of a milking machine. They are attached to a cow's teats to collect milk.

teats (TEETS)
Teats are part of a cow or other female animal. Milk comes out of teats.

udder (UH-der)
An udder is the baglike part of a cow or other animal that hangs from its belly. Milk comes from a cow's udder.